A Rationale of Textual Criticism

A Publication of the
A. S. W. Rosenbach Fellowship in Bibliography

A Rationale
of Textual Criticism

G. Thomas Tanselle

upp

UNIVERSITY OF PENNSYLVANIA PRESS
Philadelphia

Copyright © 1989 by the University of Pennsylvania Press
All rights reserved
Printed in the United States of America
Library of Congress Cataloging-in-Publication Data

Tanselle, G. Thomas (George Thomas), 1934—
    A rationale of textual criticism.

    "A publication of the A.S.W. Rosenbach fellowship
in bibliography"—Half title.
    Slightly rev. lectures delivered on Apr. 21, 23, and
28, 1987 as the Rosenbach lectures at the University of
Pennsylvania.
    Includes index.
    1. Criticism, Textual.   I. Title.
PN81.T318   1989   801'.959   88-27990
ISBN 0-8122-8173-X

For
JERRY AND SALLY

CONTENTS

Preface

THE three lectures printed here have been revised only slightly from the form in which they were delivered, on April 21, 23, and 28, 1987, as the Rosenbach Lectures at the University of Pennsylvania. My aim in these lectures is to present a rationale of textual crticism and scholarly editing, focusing first on the aesthetics that underlies textual study and then exploring in turn, in the other two lectures, the implications of that aesthetics for the treatment of documentary texts and for the production of critically reconstructed texts. Most of the points I raise have been touched on repeatedly during the two and a half millennia of recorded textual scholarship in the West: the issues have not changed, though the approaches to them have fluctuated. But I shall not here attempt a historical account or engage in debate with particular scholars, for the questions to be discussed are ones that must logically be faced, regardless of which writers have previously taken sides on them. Those questions, after all, are not simply the concern of specialists; they are of fundamental importance to all who read books, or attend lectures and plays, or listen to music and folk tales, or watch dances and films, or use printed and written matter in their daily lives.

ONE
The Nature of Texts

W HEN Keats, reflecting on the Grecian urn, wrote
that it could "express / A flowery tale more sweetly
than our rhyme," he was provoking us to consider the
difference between pictorial art and works made of words.
By calling the urn a "historian," he made clear that he was
concerned with it as a link to the past, not simply as an
object appearing before his eyes in the present. The urn had
been preserved through "silence and slow time"—and, he
said, it could "thus" express the flowery tale more sweetly,
more satisfyingly to the imagination. In so connecting the
urn's survival through time with its power of expression, is
he only telling us that his rhyme is less good a historian
because it provides a derived account and is not the primary
evidence? Or is there also the implication that even a poem
contemporaneous with the urn would be less satisfactory
than the urn because the medium of poetry necessitates a
different kind of passage through time? Keats does not
comment on the inevitable deterioration of the urn, empha-
sizing instead its enduring presence, and rightly so: if the
urn becomes discolored or chipped, we still have what is left

of it directly in front of us. But do we ever know where a poem is? Can the artifacts that constitute our evidence for the existence of a poem provide us—as the urn does—with a means for ordering the randomness of life?

Although the "legend" depicted on the urn is "leaf-fring'd," it is not a part of nature, however naturally it may have grown out of the anguish of its creator and however readily it may reflect what we believe to be the environment that nurtured it. The serenity of the immobile urn belies the teeming energy from which it emerged; in spite of the turbulence depicted on its surface, it appears tranquil in its provision of a framework for the arrangement of emotions. "All breathing human passion far above," Keats says, for the urn has presented us with an enchanted space, where boughs cannot shed their leaves and actions are frozen outside of time. This "silent form" is a "friend to man," allowing one—from the contemplative distance of art—to find patterns, and thus truth and beauty, in what had seemed the chaos of life. Poems, too, like all works of art, can serve this function. But where do we find them? Do we find poems in artifacts? Is a poem what appears in an author's final manuscript, or in a first printed edition, or in a revised second edition? Or are these artifacts records of human striving, never quite giving us the works that transcend the daily efforts of survival? Is Keats suggesting that the urn is to be favored because its palpable stasis elevates it over works that cannot be directly apprehended? Is he then claiming that the urn is well-wrought for reasons different from those adduced by later critics who find that poems can be verbal icons? But do not manuscripts and printed books possess the same passivity as other inanimate objects, and may not their texts—however unfinished or incorrect their producers might consider them—offer the same satisfying remoteness that works of visual art do? If so, what is the relation between the reading of the various documentary texts of a poem and the experiencing of the work, or are they all separate works? Such questions, like the cold pastoral of the urn itself, tease us out of thought, for they reflect the insoluble enigmas of aesthetics. And they raise issues that textual critics must not fail to confront.

Literature poses particularly perplexing aesthetic questions, for the corporeal reality of literary works has been, and remains, a matter of dispute. If we are not concerned with literature as an inheritance from the past, however, many of these questions are of little significance (and, as the formalists of the twentieth century have shown, it is not absolutely necessary for us to be so concerned—except to the extent that we must know a language, and perhaps the history of its words, to read literary works). If, for example, we think not of "works" (a term that implies previously created entities) but only of sequences of words that have come our way, links in the endless chain of language, the question of authenticity is meaningless (a point I shall return to later). But for anyone approaching a verbal statement (in the way Keats approached the urn) as a communication from the past, its location in space and time is the most basic of considerations: one must be able to distinguish the work itself from attempts to reproduce it. A work, at each point in its life, is an ineluctable entity, which one can admire or deplore but cannot alter without becoming a collaborator with its creator (or creators); a reproduction is an approximation, forever open to question and always tempting one to remedial action. Equating a reproduction with the work it aims to copy is incoherent, for an interest in works is a historical interest, and copies are the products of later historical moments. A reproduction may of course be regarded as a work in its own right, but the historical focus has then shifted. Artifacts can be viewed both as works in themselves and as evidence for reconstructing other works, but this dual possibility in no way lessens the conceptual gap between the two historical approaches to artifacts.

For those interested in recovering verbal statements from the past, the question of whether words on a page are works or attempted reproductions of works is not, on one level, difficult to answer. Even the most unsophisticated readers have sometimes decided that a particular formation of letters or sequence of words—apparently meaningless in the language being used or inappropriate in context—is a "typographical error" or a "slip of the pen," and in so doing they have perhaps faced more aesthetic issues than they knew. They were first of all showing that they wished to understand what was intended by someone else. Whether or not this goal was attainable, they had set it as their object, rather than the free play of intellect in giving the text whatever meaning suited their own experience and temperament. Then they were implicitly claiming that they had been able to locate the real work—the real statement, though not necessarily the real or only meaning—hovering somehow behind the physical text, which had served as an occasionally unreliable, but always indispensable, guide to it. They were also recognizing that what they had recovered (or attempted to recover) was not simply someone's thoughts but the actual expression of those thoughts—that (whatever we take the relation between thought and language to be) verbal works or statements are thoughts employing particular arrangements of words as their ultimate medium. Most people seem to realize that slips can occur in all kinds of verbal communication; for "literature," however we may choose to distinguish it from other verbal messages, shares some family traits with its homelier relatives. Whether one is listening to a friend, a radio announcer, or a poet, or reading a postcard, a newspaper, or a novel, one transforms the seemingly erroneous and nonsensical into the seemingly correct and meaningful—and thus implies that the verbal statement is not coequal with its oral or written presentation. Not only philosophers but all who use language have at times concluded, in one way or another, that verbal constructions are abstractions, not bound by the shortcomings of their spoken or inscribed texts.

Commonplace as this perception is, it has had remarkably little effect on the way people respond to texts. Readers' suspicions of textual corruption come in all degrees of sophistication, for the detection of error depends both on knowledge and on insight; and what one reader recognizes immediately as a misprint, another lacks the background or the talent to notice. Textual critics—that small band of historically minded readers for whom every word and every punctuation mark are suspect—stand at the opposite end of a continuum from those casual readers who, however inattentive, spot typographical errors from time to time. That such a range of readers exists is not surprising; the striking fact is how many ostensibly serious readers, including literary critics and professional students of literature, take their places in this continuum near the end occupied by the textually unsophisticated. Everyone may be aware of the potential existence of typographical errors, and a great many people also understand that texts of the same work may vary as a result of alterations, both intentional and inadvertent, introduced by the author or by others involved in the production of those texts. Nevertheless, most readers proceed to the reading of individual texts as if such troublesome facts had never entered their minds, accepting the texts in front of them with naïve faith. Critical sophistication in the extracting of meaning from words on a page can—and frequently does—coexist with the most uncritical attitude toward the document itself and the trustworthiness of its text.

This split between the activities usually called "literary criticism" and those traditionally labeled "textual criticism" is symptomatic of a widespread failure to grasp the essential nature of the medium of literature. Those who believe that they can analyze a literary work without questioning the constitution of a particular written or oral text of it are behaving as if the work were directly accessible on paper or in sound-waves. That a work of literature can be apprehended either by eye or by ear, however, should be a persuasive indication that its medium is neither visual nor auditory. The medium of literature is the words (whether already existent or newly created) of a language; and arrangements of words according to the syntax of some language (along with such aids to their interpretation as pauses or punctuation) can exist in the mind, whether or not they are reported by voice or in writing. Although the communication of literary works requires such vehicles as sound waves or the combination of ink and paper, the works do not depend on those vehicles for their existence: it has often been pointed out that a literary work is not lost through the destruction of every handwritten, printed, and recorded copy of it, so long as a text remains in someone's memory. We may doubt the accuracy of memory, but so should we doubt the faithfulness of sound recordings and of inscribed or imprinted texts.

These observations can be accepted regardless of the position one takes concerning the origins of, or the relationships between, spoken and written language or the relation of what we call language to what we call the world—for they presuppose only that a language can use both oral and visual signals, not that one of the two is primary or that meaning is derived from them by one mechanism rather than another. Nor are these points altered by the existence of works, usually called literary, that combine words with visual effects—for those works then become works of visual art as well. Furthermore, recognizing that all written or spoken texts of a work may be approximations, more or less exact, does not necessarily presuppose a concern with authors' intentions, nor does it imply that literary works are unrealizable entities (though we can never know when they are realized). It is simply the logical corollary to the recognition that literary works do not exist on paper or in sounds. Whatever concept of authorship one subscribes to, the act of reading or listening to receive a message from the past entails the effort to discover, through the text (or texts) one is presented with, the work that lies behind. Even if one denies the idea of individual authorship altogether, one still measures each text against the potentialities of the language in which it is expressed and makes adjustments accordingly, postulating in effect an impersonal intention inherent in the usage of a linguistic community. Because a literary work can be transmitted only indirectly, by processes that may alter it, no responsible description, interpretation, or evaluation of a literary work as a product of a past moment can avoid considering the relative reliability of the available texts and the nature of the connections among them.

Literature shares some aspects of these difficulties with other arts, but it is unique in the congregation of issues raised by the problem of its ontology. Aestheticians have proposed many ways to distinguish the arts one from another, but their endeavor has neglected the textual approach: why textual problems take different forms in different arts and how the significance of emendation shifts with the media. All works of art have texts, whether usually called by that name or not, for they all consist of arrangements of elements; and all can be the objects of emendation, for those elements (or their arrangements) can always be altered, producing different textures. When the creator of a work makes changes in it, they are usually spoken of as revisions. Emendations are what other people, sometimes with scholarly aims and sometimes without, do to a work in an effort to make it more nearly conform with some standard they have in mind. Any alteration, no matter who makes it (and regardless of its extent), produces what in some instances may be thought of as a new version of a work and in other instances may be considered a separate work. How, or whether, to distinguish versions from independent works is a puzzling, but subordinate, question; before one is prepared to address it, one must confront the meaning of the act of alteration. One must try to understand what it means to take a pre-existing entity and introduce changes (whether repairs or innovations) into it.

Although I am raising this question in the context of aesthetics, it clearly has a broader application: when one alters a utilitarian object not to enhance its appearance but to increase its usefulness, that action either causes the object more nearly to resemble the form intended by its designer or else moves it farther away from that form. One may not care which is the case, as long as the object performs its function better. Yet implicit in each act of alteration—once one has decided to alter an object rather than leave it alone—is an attitude toward a historical question: whether the intended form is worth recreating through repair (rectifying flaws of execution as well as deterioration from time and use) or whether seeming improvements in that form should be attempted. The issue, in other words, is whether historical reconstruction or current effectiveness of operation should take precedence, when the two do not seem to coincide. There are reasons for choosing either approach:

one is not intrinsically right and the other wrong. Deciding which path to follow is therefore a prerequisite to all other decisions on any occasion when one contemplates the alteration of an object. In this respect altering a tool or an appliance is no different from altering a painting or a text of a poem (or a text of an instruction booklet for an appliance). Obviously that basic decision is not always made consciously; but if the unexamined textual life, like other unexamined lives, is not worth living, it behooves us to give some thought to the assumptions that govern our handling of the multifarious texts of this world.

Textual critics who focus on literary texts (as most people traditionally called "textual critics" have done) concern themselves in one way or another with alterations. Whether they present their work to the public in the form of editions or of essays, the force that impels their work—indeed, at one level or another the actual subject of it—is the possibility that received texts are incorrect (according to one of many conceivable standards) and in need of alteration to set them right. If we ask what it would mean to be a textual critic of other arts, we are asking what it would mean to suggest or to make alterations in the tangible records of creativity in other media. To think about this question does not require us to explain precisely what we mean by art: it does not obligate us to distinguish literature from other uses of words, music from other occurrences of sound, the "fine arts" from other appearances of paint, ink, or marble. Such distinctions can forever be debated; but, whatever value those debates may have, they are irrelevant to a consideration of the fundamental nature of textual criticism. For all artifacts—all tangible things that we have inherited from the human past, whether regarded as debris or as testimony to the human spirit—present us with the alternatives of preservation or alteration (which includes destruction), and thus with textual problems. Textual criticism—the textual way of thinking—adjudicates between the competing claims of a basic dilemma: the feeling, on the one hand, that all artifacts, by their survival, deserve our respect, either because they put us in touch with what has gone before or because we feel a social obligation to pass along intact what we have received; and, on the other, the realization that they may fail to represent, for a variety of reasons, what their producers intended or what we feel we need, and that without correction or repair they may be misleading guides to the past, and without innovative change they may seem unsatisfying. When we talk about textual criticism we can for convenience speak of "art," and of "literature," "music," "painting," and so on; but the use of these terms does not limit the scope of textual criticism to anything less than the totality of the world of artifacts.

In practical terms, the entities most likely to remain essentially unchanged from one moment to the next, and thus to serve as direct testimony to the past, are solids, not liquids or gases (despite such occasional survivals as air trapped in amber). Therefore those arts (such as painting, sculpture, and architecture) that use solids as media result in works that are also historic objects: the pieces are at once art and artifacts. To speak of variation in such works would either have to refer to the defects of reproductions (and would therefore be a trivial point) or else would require us to imagine what the works looked like at one or several past moments or how they might change in the future. These imaginings, of course, do not alter what the works are in the present. By contrast, those arts (such as music, literature, dance, and film) that depend on sequence or duration can survive only as repetitions, which in turn require instructions for their reconstitution; and whether those instructions survive into the present through human memory or in more tangible forms (such as ink on paper, or images on celluloid), the instructions for a work are not the same thing as the work itself. Because past events cannot be duplicated in every detail, regardless of the number of instructions provided, works that exist only through reconstruction will never assume precisely the same form on any two occasions. Such works are inherently indeterminate; compared with works in solid, rock-like form, they seem as evanescent and ungraspable as air and water. Variations in them arise from two sources: the instructions themselves, which may vary in different copies; and the persons recreating the works, who may differ in their interpretations of the instructions. Textual criticism, as traditionally conceived, is concerned with the first of these, with determining what the instructions should consist of. How those instructions are then understood is often thought to be a separate enterprise. But these two sources of variation are linked in many ways, raising issues in common; and the most fundamental question joining them is what range of variation can be encompassed by the concept of a single work.

There can be no prescriptive answer to this question, for the alterations that will turn a poem or a symphony into another poem or symphony (rather than variant versions of the same one) may, with good reason, be conceived differently by different people and in different situations. But thinking about the question shows how difficult it is to disentangle the author's intention from the audience's or the performer's response, since the intention must be inferred by those who perceive the work. Performers of sonatas and conductors of symphonies need not necessarily be concerned with composers' intentions; but when they are, there is still no uniformity of result, because scores cannot provide instructions so explicit as to eliminate ambiguity regarding intention. Everyone understands that performance involves interpretation; fewer people seem to see—what should be no less evident—that the scores performers follow, not being works of music but attempts to provide instructions for producing such works, may be faulty guides and in need of correction. Interpretation of music must therefore include textual criticism; equally one can say that textual criticism of music includes interpretation, for one cannot make judgments about what should be in a score without trying to understand what the work, as a whole and in its parts, accomplishes.

As artifacts, literary texts are analogous to musical scores in providing the basis for the reconstitution of works, even though the medium of those works is different. Many people, it is true, read musical scores silently and hear the music in their minds, but such reading is only a substitute for the experience of the works themselves, which exist in sound waves. Literary works, however, need not be recited orally to be experienced as language, and all readers of literature, whether they choose to read silently or aloud, are their own performers and are recreating literary works, not substitutes for them. But despite the different relationship between performer and audience in the two arts, the act of performing music and that of reading literature both entail the interpretation of instructions, which in turn involves a critical assessment of the adequacy of those instructions. For in both these arts—and the others that must be transmitted indirectly—any textual differences that are preserved become part of the textual evidence inherited by those who follow. In their evaluation of this evidence, they struggle to distinguish errors of copying from intentional changes, and further to determine which intentional changes were made by the creators of the works and which by other people, and still further to decide which of those made by others recreate what the authors intended and which do not. As they make these decisions, they in turn produce new texts to be evaluated by their successors. This process is an inevitable concomitant to the existence of such works; and whether or not we can ever fully segregate the dual sources of textual indeterminacy in them, we must accept the fact of this indeterminacy. Various theories of literature have arisen from the premise that the *meaning* of verbal statements is indeterminate; but such theories remain superficial unless they confront the indeterminacy of the *texts* of those statements.

To speak of the textual indeterminacy of works in such media as sound, language, and movement is a very different matter from talking about the varieties of experience we have in confronting the same work on different occasions. Any work—whether tangible, like a painting, or intangible, like a poem—will produce somewhat different responses whenever we encounter it, for in each interval between encounters the unruly forces of time will have altered the work (or its physical embodiment), the present context of the work, and our own attitudes. This elemental fact is, finally, the inspiration for art, in its effort to preserve some fragments of human experience from the destructiveness of time and thus to create order out of chaos. But, being universally applicable, it is of no help in distinguishing one situation from another. The textually significant indeterminacy of the works in certain media goes beyond the omnipresent instability of the physical and emotional worlds. Whatever position we take regarding the independent existence of physical objects, we may still make a distinction between works that can survive—if they survive at all—as artifacts and works that can survive only through the instructions for their reconstitution. The former are fixed entities in a way that the latter cannot be. We have to recognize, in responding to the latter, that uncertainty is of their essence and that textual questions are integral to our appreciation of them. We can never know exactly what such works consist of and must always be questioning the correctness—by one or another standard—of the texts whereby we approach them.

By imputing relative permanence to physical objects, one is not denying that those objects do change over the years, through accretion of grime, attrition by weather, or damage from catastrophic events. And there is the further possibility that they have been intentionally altered by individuals who have touched them up here and there in an effort either to make them more consistent with current fashion or to restore them to what was imagined to be their former glory. For any of these reasons, a painting or a sculpture at a given moment is not necessarily the same as it was when previous observers saw and commented on it. Aside, therefore, from the various extrinsic elements that make every act of experiencing any work of art unique, there are intrinsic variations that affect the texts even of works constructed of tangible materials. To this extent paintings and poems raise the same textual questions: different commentators may be responding to different texts. When we hear of the cleaning of the Sistine Chapel ceiling or the Leonardo mural in Milan or the Frick Fragonards, we know that many of the details thus exposed were not available to a considerable number of the people whose recorded responses are central to the history of the reputation of these works. We also know that the appearance of each cleaned work does not exactly match the way it looked at any previous moment, even the moment when the painter stopped working on it. And if a restoration involves, in addition to the removal of dirt, the addition of paint to repair spots where earlier paint has flaked off, the result is to a still greater extent the product of the critical judgment of the person undertaking the repair. Those viewing a painting, therefore, have reason to question the text before them, just as those reading a poem do.

Nevertheless, the textual problems posed by the two situations are very different because of the media employed in the two arts. Since the work of painting is a physical artifact, any alteration in that unique physical object permanently affects the work. The painting exists at a single location, and one has nowhere else to go to find the work except that one place. Other related physical objects, such as preliminary sketches or the artist's letters, may help one understand what is in the painting or how the painting in its present state differs from what it once was or from what the artist at one time hoped it would be; but they are not sources for determining the present text of the work, for one has the work available on the canvas, and it exists nowhere else. Obviously those external documents and one's knowledge of the artist may lead one to believe that the present text of the painting is different in certain respects from what it was when it left the artist's hands; but the work is whatever is there, and one has no way of altering it short of altering the object.

In contrast, a piece of paper with a text of a poem written on it does not constitute a work of literature, and therefore any alterations one makes in the manuscript do not automatically alter the work. If one cleans a dirty spot on a manuscript and reveals a word not legible before, the word is unquestionably a part of the text of the document, but it is not necessarily a part of the literary work—nor, for that matter, is any other word in the document, for the work can only be reconstituted through the application of critical judgment to each element of every surviving text (even if there is only one, and it is the only one there has ever been). Similarly, if one touches up a manuscript by writing over an indistinct word or by marking out a word and entering another, one is certainly altering the document, but one does not thereby change the work. Such alteration of documents is regarded, by all who revere historical evidence, as a scandalous activity; but the equivalent alteration of paintings, frescoes, and sculptures is frequently advocated by responsible scholars, deeply committed to the recovery of the past. The ethics of altering artifacts shifts in the second situation because the work and the artifact inhabit the same body, and the work is considered more important.

Editors of a literary work can produce all the texts they wish, reflecting different judgments that follow from different conceptions of literature, and readers will be able to experience each of them as a work of literature—all without making any physical alteration in the documents conveying the received texts of the work, and leaving those documents as they were for future examination by others (or nearly so: any handling of a document alters it slightly). In fact, one can simply suggest textual alterations in an essay or in conversation, without actually publishing a new edition, in order to make it possible for others to incorporate those alterations into the text and experience the work in the form thus created or recreated. When scholars of the visual arts, on the other hand, form opinions about what would be required to convert a painting or a sculpture to the appearance it ought to have, according to some specified standard, their expositions in words cannot provide the aesthetic experience of a visual work; and the counterpart of what in literature and music is achieved in a scholarly edition or a textual essay—or some less formal discourse—would have to be the physical alteration of the art object itself. When there is sufficient confidence in the judgment and ability of the person proposing to alter an artifact embodying a work of visual art, those with the authority to allow the alteration sometimes do allow it, either limiting the job to cleaning or permitting retouching as well. Some regard the former as less disruptive of the artifact than the latter, even though cleaning may remove more than accumulated dirt; but both alter the documentary evidence of the inherited object. Whenever such deliberate invasion of an artifact is condoned, the underlying assumption is that in order to have the work (actually, someone's conception of what was intended by one or more of its producers) we are willing to lose part of the historical evidence that supported its reconstruction.

We cannot have both at once, as we can with literature, music, and the other sequential arts, for the work and the artifact are in battle for the same physical space. One or the other must be the victor at any moment: there can be no truces, though the triumphant work of one moment becomes the artifact of the next. The restorer of a painting and the critical editor of a literary text must of necessity differ in the impact they have on the artifacts that nourish their activity. Nevertheless, both can share the view that artifacts tell us as much about their own present state as they do about the past from which they come, and that the past can be recovered from them (to the degree that it can be recovered at all) only through an act of creative and informed judgment. In the visual arts that use solid media, the price paid for the opportunity of possibly understanding, through direct experience, works as they existed in the past is the destruction of some segment of the evidence from the past. The sequential arts do not have this constraint, but that freedom does still have its price: the inability to know what in fact any work consists of. We know what a painting now consists of, whether or not it reflects accurately what was seen in it at any previous time. It may be a damaged artifact, and we may therefore be seeing in it a fragmentary work, or it may be a restored artifact, and we may be seeing in it the restorer's idea of what the work once was; but in either case what we are seeing is indeed the work, insofar as we can experience it in the medium in which it was meant to be experienced. Because the media of the sequential arts, however, are not tangible, works in those media can never be damaged physically; but we can never know, from surviving physical artifacts, what constitutes the texts of those works. The artifacts may remain inviolate (at least as far as human intervention is concerned), but the exact contours of the works they attempt to transmit will forever be indistinct.

This difference between the two classes of art is significant whether or not one takes a historical approach to art. Talking in this way about what a work consists of may seem at first to suggest an emphasis on the form a work had at a particular point in the past and to imply that one ought to experience the work in that form. Restorers of paintings and scholarly editors of poems (as their names indicate) do focus on the past—though they have no unanimity about what past moment should be favored. Their goal is to expe-

rience each work, or version of a work, as the product of a
historical moment and to help others to have the same
experience. They would have to agree, however, that one
may derive aesthetic pleasure from any form of a work,
regardless of its pedigree: one may in fact prefer a painting
with age-darkened colors not imagined by the artist or a
poem with currently favored words substituted for the
words intended by the poet. Those who take an ahistorical
view of art are therefore inclined to believe that textual
criticism, being historical, is not relevant to their appreciation of the works they encounter; they believe that what
they bring to each work takes precedence over what follows
in its wake from its movement through time. Nevertheless,
any confrontation with a pre-existing object—any response
to an external stimulus—has a historical dimension, since
the thing responded to comes from the past, whether distant
or recent. Physics, after all, is history. (Or, if one prefers,
one can speak of unconscious, as opposed to conscious,
projections.) If we choose to accept whatever form of a
work happens to come our way—as we are free to do if we
are not concerned with its fidelity to its creator's intention
or to any other historical standard—we are still binding
ourselves to history by equating the work with that one
form of it, which is necessarily a past form. We can be
liberated from history in our aesthetic experience—if that is
our desire—only if we feel as free to alter works of the past
as to create new works of our own.

Many critics sympathetic with an ahistorical position
have not carried their arguments to this conclusion, but it

underscores the centrality of textual study even for those
not interested in history. One's response to a work is obviously conditioned by the text of it one encounters; a painting after cleaning and retouching, like a poem after a
scholar has emended it in accordance with the poet's sup-
posed intention, will produce a different response from
other texts of the same work. Those persons wishing simply
to have an aesthetic object to respond to and analyze may
not be willing to consider other texts of the work that have
existed in the past or that are now set forth as the products
of historical research; but if they see, as they must, that their
responses would be different if the text were different, they
cannot avoid questioning the text even if the basis for altering it is their own preference rather than historical evidence. The act of interpreting the work is inseparable from
the act of questioning the text.

We are thus brought back to the differing status of what
it means to question the text in different arts. We can
forever speculate in essays and in conversations about the
texts of a painting or a sculpture at various times in the past
or about what we wish they had been, but we have the
painting and the sculpture to look at and can at least see
what their texts are in the present. Or what we think they
are: although no two of us may see an object the same way,
still we are responding directly to what we believe to be a
physical object. But no text—embodied on paper or film or
in memory—of a literary, musical, choreographic, or cinematic work can serve this function because none of them is
the work. (Cinematic works, though they consist of pro-
jected light and not of celluloid, do have a physical tie that

the others do not, for a lost scene of a film, no matter how vividly someone remembers it, cannot be precisely refilmed; nevertheless, copies of film prints are like copies of printed books in their potential for variation and in their status as instructions for producing works.) Since the texts of such works are indeterminate, the point of view we take towards the nature of art will determine not simply our interpretation of these works but the very constitution of the works themselves. Whether we decide that the work is what the author hoped for, achieved, or published (in collaboration with others), or what we now find to be effective, our position will determine the text we are discussing. Because the media of those works do not admit of their being directly transmitted in tangible form, there is no way that we can talk about such works without assuming the responsibility of deciding just what we are talking about—without in effect becoming editors, since the works exist only by virtue of our specifying, in the light of one set of considerations or another, what they contain.

Those considerations may or may not be historical. Over the centuries, the bulk of the commentary on works of art has been historically oriented, taking them as the products of the processes that brought them into being. Works were interpreted in the light of their creators' lives, milieux, and motivations. But from the eighteenth century on—and particularly in the twentieth century—there has been considerable interest in taking works as objects to be examined for their seemingly intrinsic qualities, as those strike each observer, regardless of whether the perceived characteristics and meanings were intended, or could have been intended, by the creators of the works. This approach exists in various forms, some more divorced than others from the study of history; but despite the differences between the "new criticism" of one period and the "structuralism" or the "deconstruction" of another, these ways of perceiving works of art share a tendency to emphasize product over process, to focus on readers' (or viewers' or listeners') responses to works rather than on the historical forces (including authors' intentions) that shaped them. A concern with readers' responses, for instance, can be a form of historical scholarship, if its goal is to examine patterns of response at particular points in the past; but it is still directed toward works as existing entities to be responded to. Each of these approaches provides a different basis for textual decisions, and each results potentially in a different text. Paradoxically, those who are most extreme in regarding works of literature as "verbal icons" or "linguistic moments"—those most likely, that is, to think that they have freed themselves of historical constraints—are in fact tying themselves most tightly to the accidents of history as embedded in artifacts. Conversely, those most emphatic in holding that the meaning of literature emerges from a knowledge of its historical context—those most likely, that is, to believe themselves scrupulous in the use of historical evidence—are in fact hindering their progress toward their goal if they do not recognize that artifacts may be less reliable witnesses to the past than their own imaginative reconstructions.

Textual criticism is therefore basic to the critical analysis of literature (and similar arts) in a different sense from the one frequently claimed. It is often said that textual criticism is a fundamental branch of scholarship because the textual critic must provide an accurate text before the literary critic can profitably begin to analyze it. But any text that a textual critic produces is itself the product of literary criticism, reflecting a particular aesthetic position and thus a particular approach to what textual "correctness" consists of. It is true that a textual scholar can attempt to uncover, and set forth systematically, the facts constituting the textual history of a work and can stop there, without suggesting which variants might be preferred, under certain circumstances, over other variants. Such activity would indeed be preliminary to criticism (which is not to say that no judgment is involved in it), but whatever criticism followed would still have to include decisions about the makeup of the text, for those decisions are simply part of the act of reading. Anyone accepting a text uncritically—without making such decisions—is focusing not on a work but only on the text of a document. There is nothing wrong, of course, with limiting oneself to the text of a document, as long as one understands the nature of documents and proceeds accordingly. But many textual critics, no less than literary critics, have been led into muddy thinking by a failure at the outset to recognize the basic distinction between texts of works and texts of documents.

The process of reading (and thus of criticism) therefore begins with the decision whether or not to be concerned with history. One may decide not to be for various reasons: the belief, for example, that the past cannot be known; that the meanings of verbal statements are created by those who read them; that language can refer to nothing outside itself, serving (like everything else) only as material for the mind to play with. If one takes a position of this general kind, one should feel free to alter any text in whatever ways make it seem more satisfying. One would have no reason to feel limited to any inherited sequence of words, and the distinction between a work and a commentary on it would disappear. But one would still be confronting a textual question: determining the makeup of the text can never be eliminated.

Alternatively, one may decide that reading consists of attempting to receive a communication from the past. This position can be held even if one believes that objective knowledge is impossible and that we inevitably project our own attitudes into whatever we encounter. For the goal we strive toward affects the decisions we make: whether or not we can actually recover the past, setting such recovery as our aim makes all the difference, for it establishes the mental climate that enables us to evaluate the details of our world as historical evidence. And even though our principal guide to an intended text must be our interpretation of the intended meaning of the work, we can still aim for the establishment of an intended text without believing or implying that texts have single meanings. One's own sensitivity to nuances of language is then combined with what one accepts as historical knowledge in order to assess the reliability of every text—reliability according to one of several alternative historical standards, such as the author's original intention, the author's final intention, or the author's intention mediated by scribes or publishers' editors. Although any choice among these standards and any evaluation of the resulting works will inevitably reflect a critical predisposition, and thus to some extent the taste of one's own time, one's freedom to alter surviving texts is limited by what one judges the intended wording to have been—which may be far from what one wishes it had been.

This approach concentrates on the humanity of verbal statements, seeing them as the products of human agency in past moments and attempting to unlock the previous human thoughts embedded in them. The effort to understand some of the truths that other people have created for themselves (however unreachable the goal) can be a valuable part of the experience of working one's way toward self-understanding, and history can thus be helpfully involved in the individual search for order. When we encounter such products of the past as works of literature, music, dance, and film, the media of which are not physical, we can realistically hope to experience what their producers intended only through the perpetual recreation of what we believe the works to be. The details of this process may vary with the media, but the underlying issues are the same for all the sequential arts.

Textual scholars of verbal works are therefore a class of readers who make it their business to examine thoroughly the textual histories of particular works and to report those histories so that other readers may have at hand some of the information they will require if they are interested in history. When those scholars decide to produce editions, they can choose either to present the texts of documents, making no alterations in them, or else, by combining elements from different documents and admitting further alterations of their own, to prepare reconstructions of the texts of works—each of which is an attempt to recreate a given moment in the life history of a work. These two possibilities will be taken up in the two lectures that follow. But it should be clear without further discussion that, despite the usefulness of the reproduction and transcription of the texts of documents, the attempt to reconstruct the texts of works is a more profound historical activity. Although all serious students of the past have to go through this process for themselves, the reconstructed texts created by scholarly editors represent exemplary acts of reading by persons with specialized historical knowledge.

A Beethoven symphony was once described (by Edna St. Vincent Millay) as a tranquil blossom on a tortured stem. The garden of literature, encompassing every kind of writing, is filled with tortured stems, witnesses to the feverish search for shaping forms; but it also contains tranquil blossoms, which in their tranquillity show how those forms can sometimes be attained. The stems we can apprehend directly in the form of documents; but the blossoms are not so easy to see, for the insubstantial nature of language means that finished works must be searched for through the activity of mind. Some of these blossoms, when we think we have found them, will seem less beautiful to us than others, but they all have a tranquillity that comes from their being outgrowths of life, distillations of experience. It is this tranquillity that scholarly editors, when they create new texts of old works, hope to assist other readers in discovering.

TWO

Reproducing the Texts of Documents

THE evidences of human activity are everywhere around us, most noticeably in the form of artifacts, and in each of them we can, if we wish, read messages from the past. In objects that appear to be utilitarian we can try to read details of the daily affairs of those who preceded us, and in objects we suppose to be nonutilitarian we can attempt to read our predecessors' values and their sense of themselves. From both we may derive aesthetic pleasure, as their original owners may also have done, but we know when our reading of an object goes beyond what we take to be the primary purpose for which it was intended. We know the difference between praising the shape of an axe or a bowl for its efficiency and admiring it for its beauty, and we also know that any applied decoration is no less a work of art because it happens to be attached to an object of utility. When we come to objects intended to convey verbal messages, however, we sometimes fail to make these distinctions so clearly. We sometimes confuse the statement or

work with its physical embodiment, forgetting that manuscripts and printed books are utilitarian objects designed to
perform a function. Messages may be inextricable from
their media, but the medium of literature and other pieces of
verbal communication is language, not paper and ink. To
be sure, manuscripts and printed books can be objects of
great beauty, and some scribes and printers, intent on producing works of calligraphic or typographic art, may think
of the text as an element of secondary importance; but from
the point of view of verbal communication, manuscripts
and printed books are simply objects of utility. Verbal
works that make use of some of the visual aspects of written
presentation are special cases, partaking—in unequal, and
shifting, proportions—of two arts; but for the vast majority
of written verbal statements, the objects in which we find
them serve—as do all vessels—the primary function of
conveyance.

And we must further remember that inked letterforms
are part of the vessel, not its content. Once the ink is applied
to the parchment or the paper, the two are fused into one
physical object, the aim of which is to cause us to think of a
particular sequence of words. For the crystal goblet of typography and calligraphy conveys a cargo that is abstract:
letterforms provide the codes whereby we can attempt to
recreate messages. The efficiency of a document—written
or printed—in performing its utilitarian task is measured
(or would be, if such a measurement were possible) by the
degree to which the work that we think the document is
telling us to create matches the one that its producer had in

mind. Obviously, therefore, the process of reading a message as a product of the past entails the minutest examination of physical evidence, for there can be no characteristic of a document that may not have some bearing on the determination of the text of the work being conveyed.

Occasional slips of the pen and typographical errors will be recognized by some people, who will demonstrate, through their perception, that the act of deciphering documents (whether printed or handwritten, whether books or single sheets) is a creative act. The strange content of these vessels is not to be had for the asking but requires a thinking recipient who determines what is being conveyed through an analysis of all the evidence they present—evidence viewed in the light of what seems to be known of the language and the lives of those who brought the document into existence. Such analysis involves understanding the ways in which the production of a document affected the particular sequence of letterforms present in it and recognizing the alterations wrought in a document by the ravages of time. Through this analysis one moves in the direction of recovering what the producer of a document intended. If the producer was not the author of the work and if one is interested in what the author intended, then one must attempt to penetrate still further into the ancestry of what appears in the document—through a process of imaginative reconstruction rooted in what one deems to be reliable historical evidence (which may include other documents that seem intended to convey the same work).

This search, backward in time from the tangible letter-

forms in front of us, is what reading to receive communication means. Whether we are reading a scroll from ancient Palestine or a copy of an edition of a novel named in
this week's best-seller list, we are engaged in a process of
interpreting physical evidence, attempting to recreate from
it a work consisting of language. We have no choice but to
begin with the physical details before our eyes; but if we
stop there, we cannot pretend to have tried to see what these
documents, as utilitarian vessels, contain. The recognition,
however, that reading entails the active recreation of the
texts of works, not the passive acceptance of the texts of
documents, makes the physical evidence in those documents more, not less, central. Copying the text of a document produces another document; and even if (as rarely
happens) the sequence and legibility of the letterforms are
identical, the new text presents a new set of physical evidence, which cannot supersede the evidence of the earlier
document. If that earlier document is destroyed, we are then
forced to begin with the later one. We use whatever there is,
but we must use the totality of evidence each document
carries with it. The uniqueness of every written or printed
copy of a text is the irreducible basis of every act of reading.

These thoughts bring home to us with particular force the
fragility of the thread by which verbal statements hang on
to perpetual life. Those statements depend either on human
memory (and a cultural climate in which they get repeated)
or else, if written down, on the survival of documents. The
physicality of documents is comforting to those concerned
with history, for it holds out the promise that we can leap

over intervening generations and be in direct touch with the past. But the particular past moment that any document takes us to is not necessarily the one we would prefer for understanding the message being communicated. Each document is the product of so many contingencies, and its survival the result of so many more, that we must always marvel at what we have, while as students of the past we continue to lament what we have lost. In moments of flippancy, we may profess to be delighted by the destruction of certain material, for it lightens our labors as scholars. But we remain convinced, all the while, that we would have learned something from the material and would have moved a step closer to understanding a past moment. If all the lost documents had survived instead of those we have, we would feel no better off: we could not be satisfied unless we had everything. And having "everything" is an impossibility, because even if we had every documentary text of a work that ever existed, we would still not know how many other versions had once existed in its author's mind, versions that could be relevant to questioning the texts of the documents. The inherent uncertainty as to what all works made of words were meant to consist of is only exacerbated by the conditions of their transmission.

Dylan Thomas speaks of the poet writing on "spindrift pages." He may be referring in part to the immediacy of the poet's reflections, to the pages of words that burst forth like sea mist. But is he not also thinking of the evanescence of those words, created through the poet's "craft or sullen art" but destined to be ignored by the lovers, "their arms /

Round the griefs of the ages," while the words themselves begin fading into the mists of time? Certainly the conservation experts would agree that most of the materials used in the past to record words are particularly liable, if not properly cared for, to chemical decay or to the attacks of molds and insects; and at least one of those materials, acidic paper, is proving to have a life so short, when measured against the long annals of recorded history, that it is indeed but spindrift. When a document or any other artifact, defying time and chance, continues to exist—and is therefore a part of our world, as it was of our predecessors'—it will be an object of awe to those who are historically minded. No artifact can be unimportant to them, if they are serious in their historical interest, because each one comes from some time prior to the present moment and provides a connection with that time.

To revere mementos of the past is sometimes labeled sentimental or antiquarian by people who thoughtlessly repeat the cliché that to live fully we must concentrate on the present or the future and not dwell on the past. Ignoring the past, however, is not a choice that we have: to live fully presumably involves, by any definition, taking in our surroundings, making them our own, even if that comes to mean the embracing of chaos and alienation; and this process brings us face to face with the past, for everything we encounter is from the past. Our world is a world of artifacts. (Whether we choose to believe that objects owe their existence to our perception is irrelevant in this regard, for we still distinguish two levels of creativity: what we imagine that we have inherited, and what we do with it.)

Naturally there are some people whose attachment to artifacts is silly or superficial; but sentimental antiquarianism
should not give antiquarianism (or sentiment, either) a bad
name. We are all antiquarians, whether we want to be or
not, and it could therefore be said that we might as well
perform this assigned role with as much intelligence and
insight as we can produce. To show respect for artifacts is
not to advocate conservatism or traditionalism: it does not
prevent one's establishing an original relation to the universe, nor does it imply anything about the political or
social point of view one may develop. Neither does it suggest that a failure to investigate the genealogy of our environment robs our lives of satisfaction: the pursuit of history, after all, tends to reduce the seeming arbitrariness of
our surroundings, and arbitrariness does offer its own plea-
sures. Nevertheless, if our explorations among the stimuli
that seem to bombard us fail to include a historical dimension, one could argue that we are deprived of part of the
richness of human experience.

Of all the artifacts, in their wonderful diversity, that we
come in contact with, printed and manuscript materials
form one of the most significant and influential classes. Yet
many people who would readily assent to this statement
have not thought about manuscripts and printed books in
the context of artifacts in general and have not recognized
the role of artifactual evidence in understanding verbal
works. They are doubly deluded: believing that such works
actually exist in documents, and then believing that the
works can simply be poured, like so much pap, from one
container to another. Because these misapprehensions are

widespread, there has too often seemed to be a split in the world of books between, on the one side, scholars and critics (those supposedly concerned with the content of works) and, on the other, collectors and dealers (those supposedly concerned with the form of artifacts)— librarians falling somewhere in between, not sure which side to take but not doubting that there are two sides. Scholars have sometimes regarded collectors with condescension, and collectors have been all too willing to believe that they are not scholars. But anyone who comprehends how documents in fact transmit texts, and how works are related to the texts of documents, will also see that everyone in the world of books is contributing to a single great enterprise. Collectors and dealers are indeed scholars by virtue of the activity they are engaged in, for the assembling of artifacts and the ordering of them into groups that suggest patterns and relationships are scholarly endeavors. I would not claim that all dealers and collectors understand what they are doing, but then a great many scholars do not understand what scholarship is, either. The point is not whether one group has had a better record than another but that the activities they all perform are essential parts of a whole.

Descriptive bibliographers and scholarly editors would be greatly inhibited in their work if they did not have the assistance of collectors, dealers, and librarians, and they often are collectors or dealers or librarians themselves; other scholars, critics, and all other readers are likewise hampered, though they are less likely to know it, when they do not take advantage of what these people have achieved—when, that is, they do not avail themselves of the whole interconnected network of the book world. It is no reproach to anyone (to adapt a line of Housman's) not to be a descriptive bibliographer, or a scholarly editor, or a collector; specialization is inevitable, and we must at times accept—provisionally—the results of the work of others. Readers cannot be expected, every time they pick up a book, to examine all the written and printed documents relevant to the transmission of the work represented by the text in that book. But they ought to have sufficient understanding of the nature of verbal works to know that a failure to do so involves risk, and they can then judge whether, given the occasion, the risk is worth taking.

It is unfortunate that so many people still think of manuscripts and printed matter as fundamentally different from each other, or at least believe that the differences between them are more important than their similarities. One can understand why writers, readers, and officials of the mid-fifteenth century would be impressed by the promise that printing seemed to offer: the increased production of books, and in identical copies at that. But here we are in the computer age, well into the next great revolution in the reproduction of texts, acting as naïvely excited about the earlier revolution as our ancestors probably were more than five centuries ago. The "coming" of the printed book did indeed introduce a new magical object, which—for good or ill—seemed to lend authority to the text within it and stature to those who possessed it. That printed books have been a powerful force because of the mystique surrounding them—a mystique arising in part from the belief that they can endlessly duplicate the authoritative word on every subject—is a worthy theme for historical study, and it is increasingly being addressed. But if those engaged in the study are themselves under the spell of the magic, we may wonder how enlightening the results will be. And many scholars (not to mention other readers) do act as though they believed that printed books were able to defy the laws of nature, at least those that govern the human production of artifacts. In the case of printed books, they seem to think it fair to assume that examples one has not seen are the same as examples one has already looked at.

There are, of course, some readers—though not a large number—sophisticated enough to know that different editions (that is, different typesettings) of the same work are different physical objects and almost certainly exhibit different texts. But even those readers are likely to think that all copies of a single edition (which may comprise a number of separate press runs, or printings, but always from the same typesetting) are identical—identical at least in text, if not in such seemingly extraneous appurtenances as binding and dust jacket, or even title page. But is there any other instance in which a thoughtful person would claim to know the details of an object without examining it? People do not seem to be surprised when their friends' television sets or automobiles—of the same brand, model, and year as theirs—are different. But printed books (and perhaps sound recordings as well), even when similarly mass-produced, are often seen to be in a class apart, exempt from the human urge to tinker and, more significantly, from the

human inability to do the same thing twice. Persons other-
wise reasonably perceptive are often profoundly shocked by
the idea that texts in printed books (which they have not
distinguished from the texts of works) are, being made of
ink, one of the physical components of books and, like
other physical details, may vary from one copy of an edition
to another. No doubt few fifteenth-century readers, unless
they were friends of printers, knew how different from one
another the printed texts in copies of current editions
were—even though they were well aware that defective
printed sheets were often corrected or completed in handwriting and were not identical in these respects. But we—
although we may have the same desire to believe that
printed copies with identical texts can, magically, be
produced—ought to know better. Five hundrd years of in-
tensive use should have enabled us to see the printed book
somewhat more realistically.

Those who believe that copies of printed editions, unlike
manuscripts, can be identical with one another are really
thinking only of letterforms: in copies of a printed edition,
the letterforms are not individually drawn for each copy, as
they are in a manuscript. But it is a tremendous leap to
say—because a setting of type can be reused to print more
than one copy—that the copies printed from a setting of
type are in fact identical. The copies of each sheet of a
printed book are of course produced sequentially, one after
another, and are thus the products of successive moments;
what happens during, and in the interval after, the printing
of each copy of a sheet affects what will appear in the next

copy, as does the printing of that copy itself. Frequently "stop-press corrections" may take place, producing an altered text in the succeeding copies of a sheet; and other such alterations may be made when the type for other sheets is on the press. Then these varying copies of individual sheets may be gathered in many different combinations to form copies of books. Although in practice stop-press alterations (common in the first two centuries of printing) have occurred with decreasing frequency as the centuries have gone by, they can theoretically happen at any time. But their place has largely been filled, in the more recent centuries, by another procedure that can result in variant copies of books: the printing of revised leaves, or even whole sheets, and the substitution of them for the leaves or sheets originally printed. Such cancellations and substitutions often occur after some copies have been sold or distributed, releasing to the world copies that differ from the earlier copies but that do not in any obvious way proclaim their distinction. Alteration can also easily occur between press runs from the same setting of type, and often the copies of the succeeding printing are not labeled as such or distinguished in any readily noticeable way from those of the earlier printing.

Furthermore, even when there is no intentional intervention to alter a setting of type, accidents may occur to mar the printing surface, and the faulty equipment of human design may obligingly imitate its masters' habits and see to it that changes are brought about: type may shift position or drop out, and both type and plates may become damaged through wear and mishaps in such a way that some letters or marks of punctuation appear to be different ones. When one considers how many such opportunities for variation there are, one has good reason to take as a working hypothesis the view that copies of an edition will differ in text among themselves, and to reserve one's surprise for the instances when they apparently do not differ. Printed books, like manuscript books, are the variable products of human beings, who happen to have used more sophisticated equipment than pens and pencils to create them. And even when the text does not differ, copies of the same printing may vary in other ways—in the quality of the inking, in the nature of the paper or other material used as the surface to be printed, and in the way the printed sheets are assembled and bound.

There can be no identical copies of printed books, just as there can be no identical copies of manuscripts or of any other objects; but the differences in some cases may be such that one will consider them insignificant for the purpose at hand. (They may not, however, seem insignificant to another person, with other interests or greater perceptiveness.) The existence of variant texts in editions printed in the first two or three centuries after Gutenberg has become a fairly broadly known fact, but many persons who accept it still assume that nineteenth- and twentieth-century books are not plagued with such problems. The naïveté of this view can be amply documented by anyone experienced in working with these books or by many of the published descriptive bibliographies of authors from this period.

Copies do still vary, as they must, but the variations are less well known because books of the last two centuries have not yet been as intensely scrutinized for physical evidence as have earlier books. The number of known instances of variation is, in any case, beside the point. Even if no differences had ever been discovered among copies of the same editions—of any period—the point would still have to be made: since every copy of an edition is a separate physical object, there is no way to be sure what a given copy is like without examining it. The point is very simple, but it has profound implications.

One of them is that whenever any copy of any book is mutilated or destroyed, the total stock of bibliographical evidence is lessened by that much, and our ability to reconstruct the history of the edition from which it came is correspondingly diminished. No matter how large or how recent the edition, the loss of a single copy reduces the degree of certainty with which one can generalize about the edition as a whole (and therefore about the text it contains). If we care about history, in other words, we should treat every copy of every edition with the respect for physical evidence generally accorded only to books in so-called rare-book collections (institutional and private). Although sometimes even the people responsible for these collections falter (their attention causing more harm than neglect would have done), as a rule bibliographical evidence is as safe there as it can be: the point of rare-book collections, after all, is to preserve the physical forms in which various texts have appeared, and the books in these collections are more likely than other books to be housed in atmospheric conditions conducive to their longevity, at least according to the latest standards promulgated by conservation specialists.

Just how books become eligible for this friendly treatment constitutes the complex and fascinating story of trends in book collecting. A pioneering collector who breaks away from current fashions can start a new trend that results in the preservation of a whole class of previously neglected material. But however much is saved, there always remains other material in danger of destruction, because lack of demand has kept it from achieving a market value that would cause people to handle it with care. A great many copies of first printings of significant works are now in collections and relatively safe, whereas later printings and editions of those works are much less likely to be there and consequently may be difficult to find anywhere, for the traditions of collecting have not encouraged their preservation. Yet those later printings and editions contain equally valuable evidence, necessary—for example—to study the history of texts, whether one is interested in locating alterations possibly made by the author or in seeing what wording was being furnished to readers at particular times. Some later editions have exerted a far greater influence than the original editions.

It follows that all librarians and other collectors should think twice before disposing of, or rebinding, a tattered copy of any edition of any work, recognizing the grave significance of these destructive acts. When they replace a worn book with a fresher one containing the same work and think that something has been gained, they are of course deceiving themselves, for the new one—even if by a singular chance it contains an identical text—is a separate physical object, and is thus a separate witness to the text of the work it attempts to transmit. It cannot possibly be a "replacement," for one witness cannot stand in for another. How absurd, then, are those library programs (ironically called "preservation" programs) in which deteriorating books are microfilmed or photocopied and the books themselves destroyed. (The microfilming is often a necessity; the destruction of what remains of the originals never is.) A reproduction, whether produced photographically, xerographically, or in some other way, can no more be a substitute for the thing reproduced than another printed copy from the same press run can be. The idea that a work can be preserved by a reproduction of the text of one copy fails to distinguish the work from the various texts of it; and the notion that a printed text can be saved by photographing one copy fails to recognize that such a text is a part of a particular physical object and becomes something else when placed in a different physical setting. It is strange that even some people who are familiar with the history of the multiplication of copies of texts, in all its luxuriant variety, can think that their own photocopying is removed from this inexorable stream and accomplishes the physically impossible task of producing a duplicate document. Photocopying a manuscript book or a printed book creates a new document, the latest in the series of attempted reproductions of the work its text represents, a series that may include numerous handwritten copies as well as various editions with their successive printings.

All readers—that is, all of them who turn to manuscripts and printed books for texts from the past—should therefore approach these artifacts with two axiomatic points deeply embedded in their way of thinking: first, that every text has been affected in one way or another by the physical means of its transmission; and second, that every copy of a text is a separate piece of documentary evidence. The implication of the first is that reading a text with historical understanding must involve reading the physical evidence present in the same document; the implication of the second is that one can make no assumptions about the texts of any documents one has not examined, even if those documents are additional copies of a printed edition. Everyone who reads begins with physical evidence, inked letterforms on a surface; but few continue very far the process of attempting to find out what can be learned about the production of a document (and its text) from the physical clues present in it. Readers do have some assistance they can draw on: there are scholars who specialize in this kind of work (now generally called analytical bibliography) and some who incorporate the results into detailed accounts of the physical appearance, structure, and production of written and printed documents (now usually called descriptive bibliographies). Some readers feel no more impelled to consult this scholarship than to perform the work themselves; but all readers should at least understand why such work is necessary. Then when they neglect it they are making a conscious decision, on practical grounds, not acting out of ignorance of the nature of written verbal communication.

Among those readers who cannot afford to ignore this

work are—one would assume—scholars concerned with the history of books and texts. Yet, curiously enough, there are some writers on the history of printed books who believe that too much effort has gone into bibliographical analysis, wishing that some of it had instead been devoted to the study of publishers' and printers' archives. They would gladly trade a speculative conclusion drawn from the analysis of physical evidence for what they regard as a solid fact taken from a printer's ledger. Some of them also think that the close analysis of physical details is as little related to their interest in the broad picture of the influence of books on society as if it came from a different scholarly universe. Scholars who hold these views, or varieties of them, show how profoundly they misunderstand their field, and indeed the nature of scholarly research. The story of the role of books in society ultimately rests on the texts of the books and how they have been interpreted; knowledge of the variations in texts is central to the endeavor. All evidence bearing on the routines of work in scriptoria and in the printing and publishing businesses is relevant: one cannot elevate one category of evidence and disparage another. Information preserved in a firm's business records is of course part of the total body of evidence, and there is no excuse for slighting it. But the details recorded there are not necessarily the truth; they, like all other evidence, must be scrutinized with a critical eye and interpreted with informed judgment.

And when the details are of a kind that can potentially be corroborated or denied by reference to the actual books, the archives provide only secondary evidence: the archives say something *about* the books, but if the books survive they can speak for themselves. If a printer's records suggest that a book was imposed for ordinary octavo but copies of the book show that it was gathered in half-sheets, the first-hand testimony from copies of the book takes precedence over the second-hand testimony from the archives. The physical evidence in books is often ambiguous, and some analytical bibliographers have drawn unwarranted inferences from it; but these circumstances do not distinguish such evidence from any other kind of evidence, including that found in archival records. The history of the production of individual books, and the larger history of scribal practice and of printing and publishing that is built up from it, cannot be based solely on internal physical evidence; but that evidence is fundamental and cannot be ignored. Many facts about the printing practices of the past lie waiting to be discovered in the vast body of surviving printed matter, just as the operation of scriptoria, and of individual scribes, can be elucidated by the examination of the physical characteristics of manuscripts. Bibliographical analysis must be basic to any textual investigation.

Textual scholars who have thought through the nature of texts and the significance of artifacts in this way will realize, when they come to prepare an edition of the text of a document (any artifact with a verbal text, whether a personal letter or a copy of a printed edition of a novel), that they can make no alterations in that text. If they do alter the text, then of course they are no longer presenting the text of the document but are focusing on the text of the work or statement that—in their opinion—was intended by someone in the past or is more desirable in the present. This activity is often an important one (as I try to show in the next lecture), but it is an entirely different undertaking. Editors of the texts of documents will further realize that what they are attempting cannot be fully achieved: if the interpretation of a text depends in part on the physical evidence of the document in which the text appears, they must perforce deprive their readers of that evidence, for whatever kind of reproduction they make cannot be the same physical document. They can try to reproduce some of the physical features of the original and to describe others in words; but the former as well as the latter can only be reports, the accuracy of which will always be a matter of debate by those who have seen the originals.

One begins, then, with the recognition that no edition of the text of a document can be a substitute for the original and that every new edition complicates the life history of the text by releasing to the world a series of new documents. But for two reasons such editions are worth producing anyway. The first is that copies of texts (both photographic and reset) do have a usefulness as substitutes for the originals, as long as one understands their limitations. Published copies are in this way no different from private photographic or xerographic copies made for one's own purposes. The original resides at one location, but the copies can be available at many places; and recourse to the copies helps to protect the original from the destructiveness of handling. The existence of copies is thus a convenience, and at the same time it accommodates the social obligation of preserving artifacts for the inspection of future generations. These are advantages only if the users of the copies understand what it is that copies cannot communicate and know when they need to see the originals.

The second reason for the importance of editions of the texts of particular documents is that readers can take advantage of the editors' expertise. Handwritten documents are often difficult to read, both because the handwriting itself may be unclear and because the writers' alterations may be hard to follow; printed documents, too, may be misleading if they were printed from worn or damaged type or plates, and their texts, however clear, may differ from those of other copies of the same editions. In both situations—whether the document is a manuscript or a copy of a printed edition—editors who have knowledge of the writer and period in question and who have investigated the particular instance can be of considerable help to other readers. An experienced editor who transcribes a manuscript provides an expert's judgment as to what the text in fact consists of; and an editor who presents a facsimile of a printed document, having examined a large number of copies of the edition, makes an informed judgment as to which copy is the most appropriate to reproduce (and can offer a list of the variant readings in other copies).

The successful production of editions of this kind (sometimes called "diplomatic," sometimes called "noncritical") therefore requires knowledge, insight, and discretion on the part of the editor. Some people erroneously suppose that, because the editor's aim is to reproduce a text as exactly as possible, the task is a relatively mechanical one. An editor without the necessary historical background and without the intelligence and the talent to make thoughtful judgments would indeed be acting mechanically and might be better employed as the operator of a copying machine. But a published diplomatic edition must be something more than the electrostatic copy one carries away from the machine; like other intellectual products, it entails mental effort and the anguish of making decisions. The best plan for such an edition, if the documents are manuscripts (or typescripts with extensive alterations entered on them), is to provide full-size photographic reproductions, accompanied on facing pages by transcriptions and supplied (somewhere) with annotation explaining the physical details that are not evident from the reproductions. When this plan is economically unfeasible, even more annotation is obviously required to describe the physical features of the documents; but an edition consisting of transcriptions alone is clearly far less desirable than one containing photographic reproductions as well. If the documents are printed copies or fairly clean typescripts or printouts, there is no sensible alternative to reproductions, for transcriptions would serve no positive function and would take the reader farther away from the documents; the annotations in these instances, in addition to supplementing the reproductions with physical description, should identify and describe the other copies examined (carbon copies of typescripts, printed copies of editions, and historically significant photocopies of either) and record the textual variants in them.

Any reproductions to be published in a scholarly edition

must be proofread against the originals as carefully as one would proofread a new typesetting, in order to minimize the places where the reproductions are misleading. There are people—and frequently they consider themselves scholars—who work entirely with photocopies, making transcriptions from them and then proofreading against them. The results ought to be recognized for what they are: editions of the texts of photocopies, not editions of the texts of the original documents. All photocopies, and copies of photocopies, are separate documents, which are likely to mislead the editor who thinks they are adequate substitutes for originals. They can be interim substitutes; but to rely on them, believing that the originals need not be checked before an edition goes to press, is to display a profound misunderstanding of the nature of documentary evidence.

However difficult some of the decisions may be that documentary editors must make, the goal they are working toward would seem to be straightforward: the presentation in published form of texts that are as close as photography or typography allows to the texts that have survived in particular documents. Yet one continually encounters editions of letters, diaries, and other private papers in which transcriptions (often not accompanied with photographs) incorporate numerous editorial alterations (often not recorded in notes). The changes are likely to involve modernization of punctuation, such as the deletion of dashes that follow periods or the shift of commas from one place to another. This kind of tampering is claimed by its perpetrators to be for "the reader's convenience," and they say that the meaning is not affected. But the reader's convenience is

totally irrelevant, as is the fact that the editor sees no difference in the meaning. The text of the document is whatever it
is, and any alteration to smooth out a presumed difficulty
creates a different text. A reader who has been promised the
text of a document can only be inconvenienced by a text
that is intentionally inaccurate.

Just what meaning each reader will draw from punctuation, or any other feature of a text, cannot be predicted;
the purpose of preserving as many as possible of the details
found in a documentary text is to make available maximum
evidence for the use of readers. There is no detail that is not
potentially significant for interpreting meaning and assessing the writer's frame of mind. Some characteristics of a
manuscript text, such as the hurried or careful formation of
letters, cannot readily be reflected in a transcription, but the
spelling and punctuation, as deciphered by the transcriber,
can be. Handwritten and typewritten materials often contain textual deletions and insertions as well, and not to print
the deleted matter or note which words were inserted is to
misrepresent the documentary texts. The messiness of such
documents is an essential part of their nature, and a documentary edition is not performing its function if it does not
report as much of that untidiness as photographic reproduction, typographic transcription, and supplementary
discussion can convey.

All these points follow from the decision to prepare an
edition that focuses on a text as it appears in a particular
document. But of course one can also decide to focus on the
text of the work represented by that documentary text (and

possibly by several other documentary texts as well), and the result will ordinarily be quite different. Every artifact that carries a verbal text can obviously be treated either way: one can accept a surviving text as it stands; or one can alter it so that it conforms more nearly with some standard, such as what one imagines to be the text intended at a particular moment by one or another of its producers. If there were world enough and time, this decision would not have to be made, for every text could be accorded multiple editions of both kinds. But in the world we inhabit, with artifacts so plentiful and the individual lifetimes available for their study so scarce, the vast majority of documentary texts will never be the subject of editions, and most of those that are will be edited only once. No edition ever eliminates the need for further editions of the same text or work, but only those texts or works perennially deemed of the highest significance are likely to be re-edited by successive genera-tions. It becomes necessary, then, to decide in each instance which kind of edition has the greater claim to one's time and to a publisher's resources.

Taking these considerations together, one could argue that the relevant distinction is that between, on the one side, writings of the kind usually intended for private purposes (such as letters, journals, memoranda, and drafts of essays, novels, or poems) and, on the other side, writings of the kind normally intended for public distribution (such as apparently completed novels, poems, plays, and works of nonfiction prose in all fields). The former—the private writings—would seem to be best served, as a general rule, by editions that attempt to present the texts exactly as they appear in the surviving documents, thus stressing the evidentiary value of those documents. The other category—the public writings—would seem to demand editions that attempt, through editorial emendation, to offer the texts of works, the works that are but imperfectly represented by the texts of the documents. There are times, however, when one can argue that each of these classes should be handled in the other fashion: some letters, for example, may be in effect polished essays, which readers should have the chance to experience in texts purged of the idiosyncrasies of the documents; and some poems and novels may be known through the texts of fair-copy manuscripts or scarce copies of printed editions that deserve to be reproduced as signposts of literary history. No one is served, however, by the confused thinking that leads to the belief that one can alter the text of a document and still have a documentary text, or that one can aim to present the text of a work and at the same time refuse to consider emendations drawn from a variety of sources. There is no one correct approach, but there are many approaches that invalidate themselves.

Choosing to reproduce the texts of documents is a recognition of the human drama enshrined in all artifacts. What every artifact displays is the residue of an unequal contest: the effort of a human being to transcend the human, an effort constantly thwarted by physical realities. Even a document with a text of the sort not generally regarded as art—a simple message to a friend, for example—illustrates the immutable condition of written statements: in writing down a message, one brings down an abstraction to the concrete, where it is an alien, damaged here and there through the intractability of the physical. When one tries to create a work of verbal art, one aims for perfection, for the objectivity of an independent entity, expelled from the mind to exist in a space where (one hopes) other receptive minds can find it. But the vehicles required, from neural pathways to pens and inks, are uncooperative. As a result, we have manuscripts and typescripts that exhibit authors' slips, false starts, cancellations, and revisions (and second and third revisions) or copyists' misreadings and erasures; and we have printed books that show how difficult it is for typesetters to set the right pieces of type. The world of documents is a world of imperfection. A writer may write about human striving but will probably consider the text flawed if it betrays the uncertainties and accidents of its own composition and transmission. Yet they cannot be kept out.

One may, from time to time, wish to regard a verbal document as a work of visual art, seeing it as if in an exhibition case or a frame on a wall; all the flaws in its verbal text then become parts of the composition, the blots and erasures and misprints contributing their share to the visual impact of the whole. The document, whatever state its verbal text is in, is a human intrusion into the realm of the nonhuman and can (in Eliot's words) provide "the still point of the turning world," can be like the Chinese jar moving "perpetually in its stillness," serving to organize our perceptions. But even though a document, like any other artifact, possesses this calming and nourishing stasis, we must also recognize, if we are interested in the verbal message it bears, that it reflects the pulsing and tortuous underside of stasis, freezing into inanimate solidity one moment in the history of the attempt to transmit a work made of words. Melville likened the creation of art to Jacob's wrestling with an angel. The texts of documents preserve a partial record of that struggle, and the effort to make this record more widely known is a noble service, contributing to the knowledge we have of what it means to be human.

THREE

Reconstructing the Texts of Works

THE woman walking along the Key West strand, in Wallace Stevens's poem, transmutes the sea into her song; but the two are different, we are told, "Even if what she sang was what she heard, / Since what she sang was uttered word by word." In verbal communication, everything depends on the procession of words, one by one, in sequence. When a word, or the sequence, is altered, the meaning can be expected to change. The text the woman sang may not have been the text she intended—but not because it seemed to her (as no doubt it would have seemed) an inadequate expression of the complexity of her upwelling emotions. The execution of a statement never exhausts the potentiality of the ideas underlying it. Even so, certain words were intended, but through one slip of the tongue or another some of them may have come out differently in the uttering. The assembled listeners were able in any case to recognize that her song was a made reality, a created world: they understood, as they listened, that "there never was a world for her / Except the one she sang and, singing, made." We are not told whether any of the listeners mentally corrected some of the words they heard, in the process of forming their individual interpretations of the singer's world. But what they heard did have an effect on them, altering their perceptions of their own worlds; for as they turned toward the town, the lights in the fishing boats "Mastered the night and portioned out the sea, / Fixing emblazoned zones and fiery poles, / Arranging, deepening, enchanting night." The exemplary world of her creation gave direction to the "rage for order" in each of them, helping them to find undreamed-of patterns in the chaos around them and enhancing the vibrancy of their participation in it. Textual criticism was a part of this process—even if Stevens does not say so—because the listeners had to decide whether the words presented to them were the ones that, taking everything into account, they should respond to. Each of the listeners had been presented with a text and was engaged in finding in it a work. The presented text was a historical fact; the text of the work was an imaginative construction based on it, and possibly different for each of them. But it was the work that affected them, for they were trying to understand what was being said, even if the uttered words sometimes subverted it.

Every verbal text, whether spoken or written down, is an attempt to convey a work. The preservation of the documents containing verbal texts, like the preservation of other artifacts, is a vital cultural activity. But the act of preserving such documents, unlike that of preserving paintings, for example, does not preserve works but only evidences of works. If, as readers, we are interested in the verbal works that their producers intended, we must constantly entertain the possibility of altering the texts we have inherited. Those texts, being reports of works, must always be suspect; and, no matter how many of them we have, we never have enough information to enable us to know with certainty what the works consist of. The attempt to move closer to an intended form of a work, whether it occurs mentally in the process of reading or publicly in the production of a scholarly edition, is a historical exercise. Some people, of course, do not wish to bring historical considerations to their appreciation of works of art, preferring instead to respond to works simply as objects existing in the present. When they talk about a painting from this point of view, their comments are nevertheless in response to an artifact surviving from the past; if, however, when they wish to discuss a literary work (or any other piece of verbal communication), they limit themselves to an artifact, they are not discussing the work, but only the text of it that happens to appear in the artifact. Because the medium of literature is abstract and because literary works therefore cannot exist in physical form, any attempt to apprehend such works entails the questioning of surviving texts.

This activity is necessarily a historical enterprise, for the very concept of a "work" implies something pre-existing. It is true that one cannot fully re-enact the responses of members of the original audience of a work, and one's own response will always be affected, in some degree, by the intervening experience of humanity and the climate of one's own life; but still one is responding to a creation formed by a human being (or more than one) at a particular time in the past. Persons not interested in taking any of the historical approaches to literature need not search for the work represented by the text, but they should realize that what they are doing is equating the text of the document before them with the text of a work—just as if the object before them were a painting. What they then say or write is further removed from works of literature than are the comments of similarly inclined art critics from paintings. Even if such art critics seem to be responding more to colors of paint than to works of painting, and even though the colors present at one moment are not exactly those present at another, the colors and the works coexist in the same objects. Nevertheless, both groups of critics are alike in taking the artifacts they encounter as the stimuli for flights of fancy and displays of intellect, for fantasias upon found objects. The results may or may not be works of interest, or of genius, in their own right; but they are not writings about works of art or of literature.

Once we understand that the texts of verbal documents are not the texts of works, and once we decide that we do wish to concern ourselves with works, we are then faced with the question of how to alter the texts of the surviving documents, with the task of determining what standard to aim for in making emendations. For we must have a standard, a guiding principle, in mind: there are an enormous number of ways in which we could alter and conflate the surviving texts, and we must know what stage in the history of the work we wish to reconstruct, or else our emendations will be no more than aimless tamperings. Of course, one could say that making changes according to what pleases us at the moment is itself a principle, and it could result in works that would seem to many people superior to what the original authors were capable of. But it is not a historical approach and will not help us to arrive at the form of a work intended by someone at some time in the past. (If it did, coincidentally, lead us to the same text as one produced by a historically minded editor, it would still not be a historical reconstruction, for we define our locations by the roads we have taken.) In the life story of a work, there are a vast number of moments to choose from, a number that increases as each hour goes by; and at each of those moments there may have been a variety of people affecting the text. The basic question for every reader interested in history—and perforce every scholarly editor—is to decide whose intended wording, and at what time, is to be extracted from the clues provided by the documentary text (or texts).

When A. E. Housman read over the fair copy of his funeral hymn, which contains the line "Through time and place to roam," he appended a note saying, "The printer will already have altered *place* to *space*." The sardonic humor of this comment is not unexpected from the author of *A Shropshire Lad* or from the experienced poet who had suffered through many sets of proofs. But the scholarly editor of Latin poetry is also speaking here, the textual critic who had formed the habit of questioning every text and who knew that scribes and compositors have left their traces in all the texts they have touched. His remark effectively underscores the problematic nature of tangible texts, their uncertain relation to the works that lie behind them. As matters turned out, the printed program for his funeral did include the line as he wished it to be—that is, if one takes his footnote at face value and does not conclude that he wrote it because he was undecided and half wished the printer in fact to print "space," the word he claimed to castigate the printer for imagining that he had written. If Housman's annotated manuscript had not survived, we might expect to find a learned editor of an edition of Housman's verse conjecturing that Housman no doubt meant "time and space," not "time and place," and perhaps emending the line accordingly. Printers are not the only ones who make mistakes with texts. But we would have no way of knowing, with any likelihood of certainty, that the emendation was a mistake; and the possibility of mistakes is the price we pay—and should pay willingly—for the opportunity of seeing what wording occurs to someone who has given serious and extended thought to the question.

Suppose the printer had indeed got it wrong, and suppose also that the manuscript had not survived. A number of readers, including—one hopes—an editor or two, might have suggested the right reading; but it would be only a conjecture, with no documentary support, and no one could prove that it was correct. And in what sense, even with the evidence we actually have, is it correct? If the audience at the funeral had listened to, and read, the word "space," would that word take on some authority by virtue of historical circumstance? And how do we know that the surviving document tells the whole story? Can we be sure that Housman did not later change his mind, perhaps at the urging of a friend, whether or not he wrote his revised opinion down and whether or not it has survived in physical form? And should we take "place" to be the only word that might have been erroneously altered? Might not the attention Housman directed to this word have caused him to overlook his own slip of the pen in another line? However likely or unlikely one regards any of these possibilities to be, there is no denying that the text of this simple poem, like the texts of all other poems, is a tissue of uncertainties—and will remain so regardless of the plenitude of relevant documents that may turn up.

The way one threads a path through these uncertainties—to arrive at a defensible reconstruction of the text of a work of literature—depends on the position one takes regarding two questions: what agency is responsible for the production of a work, and what point is the most significant in its history. On the former question, one may feel that the author has sole responsibility for a work and that a text reflecting the author's intention (and purged of elements contributed by others) best represents the work; or one may believe that literature is a social art, the collaborative product of a number of people, and that the text resulting from the publishing process (though cleansed of scribes' or typesetters' errors) provides the truest record of the work. On the second matter, one may decide that the form of a work most worth focusing on is the one that existed at the moment when the work was regarded as finished by those responsible for it (whether the author alone or the author in conjunction with others), a moment that may be deemed to have brought to fruition the efforts of a period of creativity;

or one may prefer the last version of a work overseen by whoever is considered to have had charge of it, a version that may plausibly be thought to incorporate maturer views and more refined phrasing than earlier versions. An intermediate stand on each of these questions may at times seem in order: one might wish to accept revisions originating with the author's friend but not the publisher's reader, or those appearing in the third, but not the fifth and last, revised edition.

Forceful arguments for these various positions have been made. But many of them come from people who act as if only one approach is correct, as if it—and only it—leads to truth. They do not recognize that, since every verbal work must be reconstructed, no text of any such work is ever definitive. Different individuals may favor different approaches, and even those taking the same approach may make different judgments. None of these approaches and judgments can be automatically ruled out: they all emphasize some stage in the history of a work, and nothing that ever happened is theoretically without interest or unworthy of our attention. What makes one position defensible, and another not, is the coherence of the argument supporting it, the way the argument fashions a whole out of what seem the fragmented facts. There is thus no one valid line: the acceptable answers are limited only by human ingenuity, even while the unacceptable ones measure the breadth of the mind's inadequacies. Arguments that contain internal inconsistencies or lapses of logic, even if they are well-informed, do not help us to find a way through chaos, for they are themselves chaotic. But those that satisfy the intellect by their effective marshaling of the apparently relevant evidence and by the harmony and coherence of their insights create visions of the past that can be accepted—until new discoveries and more trenchant analyses render them no longer necessary or compelling. With texts, no less than with everything else, we credit, and discredit, our truths in this way.

Over the years the most frequently adopted textual argument has assumed that the goal of scholarly editing is the reconstruction of texts intended by their authors. Because authorial intention can be defined in various ways and because authors frequently shift their own intentions for a work as time passes, this general rationale can support a number of interpretations. What links them all, however, is a biographical interest, a desire to learn as much as possible about the minds in which works originate. Even though verbal texts (and often the works they represent) become the joint products of several people by the time they are published (a situation as true of ancient manuscript books as of modern printed ones), and even though they employ words and rules of syntax that antedate their conception, there is still a single mind that provided the impetus for each work. Folk tales are no exception: neither the social origins of the author's sources and language nor our apparent inability to identify the author invalidates the search for the mind most responsible for shaping a work.

The claim that this view is artificial—because verbal works cannot reach audiences without the intervention of a number of people—carries no weight. As long as there is historical interest in a work, or a series of works by the same author, there must also be a legitimate interest in the author's vision, whether or not we can now uncover it and whether or not the conditions of publishing allowed it to reach an audience unscathed. The works represented by Thomas Wolfe's sprawling manuscripts and by the papers Ernest Hemingway left at his death were considered inappropriate for commercial publication until editors hired by publishers turned them into different works (or versions of works); but even if those publishers were correct in assessing the realities of the world of publishing, there is still good reason to wish to read Wolfe and Hemingway in the forms they envisioned as they wrote. Their desires have just as much historical reality as do the texts that were finally published, though the desires are likely to be harder to locate. If we grant that authors have intentions and therefore that the intentions of past authors are historical facts, we require no further justification for the attempt to recover those intentions and to reconstruct texts reflecting them, whatever our chances of success may be.

Understanding the kind of authorial intention that is relevant to textual decisions is less difficult than determining the practical results of the operation of that intention. An author may intend to write a work that sells well, or one that receives critical acclaim, or one that influences the thinking of large numbers of people, or one that has various other results. Such hopes regarding what a work will lead to are part of the biographical context out of which any work emerges; but they are not examples of the kind of intention that directly affects the reader's and textual critic's attempt to ascertain the intended text of a work. Authorial intention for this purpose must be the author's wish, in the act of composing, to have a particular word or mark of punctuation at a given place in the text.

A rigorous application of this concept enables one to make decisions in situations that have been considered difficult, and have been much debated, through a lack of clear thinking. For example, when both a final manuscript and a printed edition set from it survive, the question arises as to whether the author's intention is better represented by the oddities of usage and punctuation in the manuscript or the conventional usage and punctuation in the book. If there is a good case for arguing that the normalizing in the book text was performed by a member of the publisher's staff and not by the author, then that text could not be preferred over the manuscript text, as long as one is concerned with the author's intention. Even if the author intended to write a work that would be considered correct in its grammar and punctuation, such an intention involves the expectation that someone else will rectify any flaws of these kinds; it cannot prevent the author from intending at the moment of writing to put down particular words or punctuation marks, possibly not knowing that by the standards of the day they are regarded as unconventional.

Any so-called intention that is actually an expectation about what will be done to the text by others can have no bearing on the reconstruction of an authorially intended text. The first-edition text, often with such alterations incorporated, is naturally of historical interest, because it is the text that was made available to the public. But that is a separate historical interest from the one that causes us to be concerned with authors' intentions. Some people seem to believe that, because authors wished or expected certain things to be done to their texts, we are carrying out their intentions by doing those things or accepting texts in which they have already been done. But to take this view is to confuse two incompatible goals of textual scholarship. Of course, we can define "intention" any way we like, and the word need not be used as I am using it here. The point is not what term we use but how we segregate two distinct concepts. We need to distinguish in some way between the texts of a work as they existed in the mind where it originated and the texts of that work that contain contributions by others (some of which might perhaps have been anticipated—though not necessarily welcomed—by the author). One shorthand way of referring to this distinction is to say that the former are the texts the author intended and that the latter may in some ways conform to what the author expected.

Authorial intention, so defined, is clearly not the same thing as authorial action: what authors have in mind when they are writing and intend to write down is not necessarily what they do in fact write down, through carelessness, a preoccupation with the next phrase, or any kind of momentary distraction. Distinguishing intention from expectation, therefore, does not involve equating the text of a document with that of a work, since even the text of the author's own finished manuscript may not be the intended text of the work. The scholarly editor must be prepared to make alterations in any documentary text if the goal is to arrive at the author's intended text. Furthermore, defining the intended text as what was in the author's mind at the time of writing does not preclude accepting revisions by the author. Like other people, authors can be expected to change their minds; and whether they write out whole texts when they make revisions or enter the revisions on pre-existing documents or hold them in their minds, the intention underlying the altered phrases is of the same order as that underlying the previous version of them. The result is more than one intended text of a work, and the scholarly editor has to decide which one to focus on—at least, which one to focus on first. All are of interest, but the editor, more often than not, aims to produce only one edition of a work; indeed, the publication of one edition may for a time make the publication of others seem an unattractive proposition to publishers, except for works considered at the moment to be of the highest importance. The choosing of one of the intended versions of a work over another may thus be dictated by practical considerations, but the actual choice is likely to reflect, more substantively, the nature of the surviving materials and the editor's literary and historical judgment.

We depend on the survival of documents for the evidence that makes the reconstruction of versions of works feasible, but we must be careful, in thinking about versions of works, to observe the distinction between the texts of documents and the texts of works. Even if scholarly editors could emend the texts of surviving documents perfectly so as to remove all nonauthorial elements, the result would not

necessarily be the texts of versions of works that ever existed as versions in their authors' minds. Certain indisput-
ably authorial revisions that first appeared in public in a
fourth edition, for instance, may have been present in the
author's mind at the time of the third edition and intended
for inclusion in that edition, but left out through the publisher's (or even the author's) oversight. If one were interested in the version represented in general by the third
edition, one would have to try to identify such fourth-
edition readings and emend the third-edition text with
them; although the earliest surviving documents in which
those readings happen to appear are copies of the fourth
edition, the readings were not part of the new revision
undertaken for that edition. Those editors who maintain
that they cannot take readings from different editions because they do not wish to mix versions together—and there
are such editors—have failed to understand how the texts
of documents are different from the texts of works. Editors
of ancient works—who of necessity deal with manuscripts
written many years or centuries after the authors' deaths—
are less likely to make this mistake than editors of more
recent works (though they may be more likely to neglect the
possibility that variants might reflect authorial revisions).
No one whose aim is the study of versions of works as
intended by their authors wishes to mix elements of different versions together; but we must remember that versions
are what we are setting out to reconstruct, not what we
have been handed on the platters that documents provide.

Some stages in the history of a work can be eliminated

from consideration more quickly than others. Some, for example, may seem so conjectural, for lack of surviving evidence, that one may feel one's time better employed by concentrating on a stage for which the evidence is more plentiful. And some stages may never have been represented visually or in sound recordings at all: a version of a work—not just the idea for a work—can exist in its author's mind without being written down or recorded, as when an author has thought of a number of revisions for a new edition but dies before making note of them and before the new edition is called for. Such versions had a real historical existence but are now unrecoverable. Of those that seem recoverable, some may be judged less desirable to present as reconstructed texts on the grounds that they appear to us, looking back as historians, to be preparatory to more climactic versions. Although every revision can be regarded as producing a new work, in practice some revisions will seem more transforming than others: some seem to refine the expression of a passage without changing the drift or general effect of the whole, whereas others (not necessarily more extensive) seem to metamorphose a work into what one can only call a different work, despite the many sequences of words it still has in common with the earlier one. When it can be argued that a particular stage of revision, or series of stages, is of the first kind, refining but not transforming the work, one may feel that the version resulting from these revisions should be focused on, out of respect for the author's right to make alterations. But when a revision is of the second kind, creating what may be thought of as a new work, one may decide not to focus on it, preferring instead—for historical or literary reasons—the prior version. One might choose an early version of Henry James's *The American*, for instance, rather than the revision for the New York Edition thirty years later. Such a decision does not violate the author's intention by failing to emphasize the last revision, for it recognizes that two versions may embody two incompatible intentions and must then be treated independently.

All these decisions obviously depend on the editor's historical interests and literary taste. One sometimes hears complaints about the subjective element in editing, and there is a long tradition, perhaps most often reflected among those editing ancient writings, of searching for a procedure that eliminates human judgments. No such system has been found, of course, nor will it be. But textual criticism is not the only realm of life in which dreams of a certainty independent of our perception have proved hard to resist. We should instead embrace the inevitable and concentrate on defining the role of judgment in each undertaking. One example of confused thinking on this score is the reluctance some editors feel to admit into a text revisions that they cannot regard as improvements. These editors often seem to be taking as their motto Umberto Eco's remark, "The author should die once he has finished writing. So as not to trouble the path of the text." Authors' revisions do complicate those paths—and editors' work. But we should not be troubled by revisions that seem to reflect authors' lapses of taste or their lack of attention to context, if those revisions appear to be the facts of history. As long as our concern is with authors and their intentions, we cannot reject revisions made by authors simply because we consider them misguided, for we are then placing ourselves, not the authors, at the center of attention. It is not a coherent argument to profess to be interested in works as the products of individual authors and then to maintain that editors must come to the rescue of authors and save them from their own bad judgments. The flaw here is not the subjectivity involved, for historical commentary cannot avoid interpretation; the problem is the failure of the argument to reflect an awareness of the historical nature of the judgments required. It is not the editor's own literary preferences that matter but the editor's literary sensitivity channeled to the solution of a historical problem: the determination—to the best of one's informed judgment—of what text of a work the author considered to represent that work most satisfactorily at a given time. Any other focus turns the endeavor in a different direction, away from the author.

One can never, of course, fully isolate the author from all influences. Language itself is an outside influence, a set of inherited conventions shared with a community, and writers can depart from those conventions—in order to achieve special effects—only up to a point if they are to be understood. Writers, like other people, are further influenced by conversations they engage in and by what they read and look at and listen to: influences that are part of the act of living, part of the experience that inspires writing. But there is another kind of influence that occurs when someone reads or hears a text and makes recommendations for re-vision—sometimes gently, sometimes insistently—to the au-thor. If the author accepts the suggestion of a friend or feels under pressure to follow the demand of a publisher, the result is a text altered through outside influence. This kind of influence, directly affecting an already-formed passage, is the only kind that an editor can try to counteract. There does exist, it is true, such a thing as collaboration, in which two or more people create a work, or a passage, in a process of harmonious give-and-take that resembles the working of a single mind. One must be extremely cautious, however, about interpreting a writer's acquiescence in the proposals of others as instances of true collaboration. Writers have many motives for agreeing to changes that they do not really desire, and their own statements on the matter, which are often attempts at self-persuasion, cannot be accepted uncritically. Even though it may not be easy at times to draw the line between interference and collaboration, or even between the sort of influence that directly alters an existing text (as both interference and collaboration do) and the sort that becomes one of the author's sources for the work, these distinctions are essential if one is to take any kind of historical approach to verbal works.

After the distinctions have been attempted, one obviously need not give preference to an author's intention, for what is done to a text by the author's friends, scribes, printers, and publishers is also a matter of history, and one can decide to reconstruct the version of a work resulting from the ministrations of any of them. Such a goal is as valid as that of recovering the author's intended text: each is valuable and serves a different historical purpose. And they cannot be pursued simultaneously, either, for the textual intentions of authors and publishers are so likely to move in different directions that no single text can accommodate them. Lord Dunsany could think of no higher compliment to pay Elkin Mathews than to say, "I used to forget with him the natural antagonism that the business of publishing necessitates except in rare cases, between author and publisher." The textual situation is not essentially different for theatrical works, though one may be tempted to think that true collaboration more often exists between playwright and director. But a dramatist may agree during rehearsals to textual alterations, given the actors and director present at the time, without believing the changes to be improvements—just as a novelist may accede to a publisher's request for alterations without losing faith in the unaltered text. Terrence McNally, for instance, once expressed concern about whether he could "guard the vision" of his plays during actors' readings and rehearsals ("I worry," he said, "that in the process of developing my new play I lose it"). Playwrights have been known to accept revisions in performances of their plays that they do not incorporate into the published texts; but even if a playwright does make a reading text conform with a performance text, there is still reason to be interested in the text as it stood before rehearsals began. The fact that plays as produced are collaborative efforts does not mean that plays as written—plays as they left their authors' desks—are not works of drama, worthy of study as art.

The products of creative individuals, before they are altered by those whose job it is to bring such works to the public, are always of interest. But the form—of a play or of a novel—that reached the public, often not the author's in many respects, is also of interest because it is what was available for people to read and be influenced by. Successive editions of a work, both during its author's lifetime and later, often become the most available texts in their turn. If one wishes to understand the comments made about a work in the past, one needs to know not what text or texts were intended by the author but what texts each of the commentators read. Some of these texts may no longer be extant and can be known only through reconstructions, the evidence for which may be limited to what is found in the commentaries themselves; others may have survived and can be studied with the assurance that one is looking at the same text that some readers of the past also looked at. The textual historian, determining what texts of a work have existed, establishes the range of texts from which a given commentator could have drawn. This brand of textual study is concerned with the public life of texts, with the way texts affect, and are affected by, the stream of history.

Ezra Pound professed to be content with the alterations—not of his own devising—that crept into his *Cantos* as they made their way through the publication, and republication, process, because they were a part of its encompassing of history; he thus appeared to be abolishing textual error by enveloping the marks of the poem's own vicissitudes into its artistic design. But in fact he was only approving what he was powerless to prevent—not that he was powerless to express his intentions when marking proofs but that, like every other author, he could not fully control what finally appeared in the published text. Every text that leaves its author's hands takes on a life of its own, whether with its author's blessing or not. Pound's incorporation of the accidents of history into his stated aims for his work does not mean that we should lose interest in the work as he created it. Nor does the contrasting view of most writers—that alterations they did not initiate threaten the artistic integrity of their works—provide any justification for our slighting the versions of works containing nonauthorial elements. All versions of a work that once existed are legitimate subjects for historical reconstruction, but each reconstructed text can only be an attempt to bring back one of them.

Determining the stage that one wishes to recapture in the history of a work is a separate matter from deciding how best to accomplish the task. If one has chosen to concentrate on the social product—on the work as it emerged from the collaborative process that leads to publication or distribution—one might well conclude that the most appropriate text need not necessarily entail reconstruction at all but might instead be one of the texts actually published. A published text is of course not quite the same thing as the text intended by the publisher. In the case of a printed edition comprising variant copies as a result of stop-press corrections or the substitution of corrected leaves or sheets, one might indeed wish to reconstruct a text incorporating all the corrections found in different copies. Such a text would be the most correct form of the published text but could still contain what from the publisher's point of view were errors. Nevertheless, each of the variant published texts, however it may have fallen short of the publisher's intention, has the advantage of displaying one form of the text that was in fact offered to the reading public. Naturally one could try to reconstruct a text representing the work as affected only by the author's friend or literary adviser or printer or publisher; but, unless one of those persons were of particular renown and interest, such reconstructed texts would have less practical usefulness than a text showing the cumulative result of all their contributions. Even though the published text might contain readings not intended by any of them, those errors would be part of the text presented to readers, and thus relevant to the concerns of those who see verbal works as collaborative products. Their approach leads inevitably in the direction of favoring the texts of documents, not the reconstructed texts of works, as the material of historical study.

It is for this reason that discussions of scholarly editing often concentrate on authorial intention—not because collaborative texts are necessarily considered inappropriate but because they can frequently be represented by the texts of existing documents, whereas texts reflecting authors' intentions are more likely to be ill represented by any surviving documentary texts and to demand reconstruction. Editors of ancient works sometimes claim that the best they can do in each case is to reconstruct the text of the manuscript that was the common ancestor of all the surviving manuscripts, a text that may be very different from the one intended by the author. This position, however, exaggerates the distinction between assessing the variants present in documents and offering new readings not present in any document. The former carries no greater certainty than the latter, both being the product of informed judgment, which can have the author's intention as its aim just as readily as the scribe's intention. Editors of works written from the late Middle Ages onward—works, that is, generally represented by texts contemporaneous with their authors—have less hesitation to take authorial intention as their goal; but their attention to it is sometimes deflected by the allure of certain documents sanctioned in one way or another by the authors. Thus an editor may be tempted to adopt the conventional punctuation of a first-edition text rather than the idiosyncratic punctuation of the author's manuscript, forgetting that to do so would be to elevate authorial expectation or acquiescence over authorial intention, and therefore to shift the focus from the individual author to the collaborative group.

Given the rarity of accurate copying, the best guide to authorial intention is likely to be the author's own final manuscript, or in its absence the manuscript or printed edition derived from it with the smallest number of intermediate steps. Authorial revisions from later texts can of course be incorporated into that early text, depending on what stage in the history of the author's changing intentions one is concentrating on; and there may be instances where an author has so thoroughly worked over a text that—in the absence of a new manuscript—a later edition can become the point of departure for reconstructing the text of a revised version. Determining which variants are revisions intended by the author is the heart of the editing process and requires editors to survey all available evidence—the physical evidence present in each textual document and any other relevant historical evidence outside those documents—and to evaluate it with sensitivity and good judgment. The result is a historical reconstruction, even though it may not correspond with any text that ever existed in tangible form, because the goal is what once existed in the author's mind. The validity of the reconstruction rests entirely on the quality of thought engaged in its preparation.

With this framework for thinking about the reconstruction of texts, one can see how various issues fall into place. Whether, for example, an editor should enforce consistency in punctuation and spelling depends on the author's intention or the conventions of the time, whichever is being emphasized. More often than not over the centuries consistency in these matters has not been regarded as something particularly worth striving for. Other forms of modernization must also, by definition, be avoided in a historical reconstruction. The alteration of punctuation and spelling to make them conform to a presumed present-day standard should be thought of in the same terms as translation or any other kind of adaptation for a particular audience. Unconscious modernizing is bound to occur, for whatever one does reflects the workings of a mind conditioned by the present; but the pursuit of history, which appears to be one of the distinctive urges of the human mind, requires us to attempt to put ourselves in tune with minds of the past. We may be relatively successful or unsuccessful in reaching this goal (and we shall never know which), but having such a goal is a very different proposition from deciding deliberately to adapt a past statement to present custom.

Modernizing the nontextual elements of the documentary presentation of texts, however, is outside the scope of textual criticism and can only be judged according to one's standards of graphic design. What is nontextual in each instance depends on how one interprets the author's (or someone else's) conception of the work. Some visual features, such as poetic lines and indentations (or even poetic shapes and typographic patterns), may be textual, when others, such as typeface designs, are not. Authors can have firm opinions about book design and play a role in designing their own books but still not think of typography as an element in their works. They may also take for granted a particular form of presentation, but such an expectation does not in itself mean that they consider that form integral to their work. Of course, some do, and their works must then be approached as works of visual as well as verbal art. (They would then be analogous to woodcuts, etchings, lithographs, photographs, and the like, as tangible works that are intended to exist in multiple versions, each of which is a separate physical object inevitably exhibiting individual characteristics.) It is true that every aspect of the design of a document—such as the quality of paper, the dimensions of leaves, the style of letterforms and layout, and the widths of margins—can influence readers' responses to the text it contains; conventions in these matters do become established, and readers learn to read many of the visual attributes of documents in addition to the visual representations of words and pauses. If one is studying

readers' responses of the past, therefore, one must take all
such characteristics of documents into account; they are all
obviously part of the documentary evidence that scholars
must examine. But if one is reconstructing texts intended by
their authors, one generally need not preserve these features
of documents, for they are not, except in unusual cases, part
of the intended texts.

Of all the historical activities of textual study, the effort
to reconstruct the texts of works as intended by their creators takes us deepest into the thinking of interesting minds
that preceded us. We must respect the documents that make
our insights possible, but we cannot rest there if we wish to
experience the works created by those minds. The old man
in Yeats's poem, who in sailing to Byzantium is voyaging
out of nature and into art, understands how human creativity liberates the soul from its bondage to deteriorating flesh.
The soul must "clap its hands and sing, and louder sing /
For every tatter in its mortal dress"; but it can learn how to
sing, Yeats says, only by "studying / Monuments of its own
magnificence." Even if one believes that Yeats overstated
his case and that there are other kinds of singing schools,
one can still recognize the positive values inherent in the
attempt to recover the past. One has no obligation to look
backward, if one's temperament does not allow the looking
to enhance one's sense of human possibilities and of self-
fulfillment. But neither should one feel a necessity to try to
ignore the past, out of a belief that only by so doing are
one's human potentialities freed. What is perhaps most
distinctively human is the acceptance of alternatives, the
recognition that no single point of view can adequately

encompass the attitudes of human beings about their own existence. One of those alternatives is what textual criticism offers, the search for past intentions in all their rich complexity.

Our cultural heritage consists, in Yeats's phrase, of "Monuments of unageing intellect"; but those monuments come to us housed in containers that—far from being unageing—are, like the rest of what we take to be the physical world, constantly changing. Verbal works, being immaterial, cannot be damaged as a painting or a sculpture can; but we shall never know with certainty what their undamaged forms consist of, for in their passage to us they are subjected to the hazards of the physical. Even though our reconstructions become the texts of new documents that will have to be evaluated and altered in their turn by succeeding generations, we have reason to persist in the effort to define the flowerings of previous human thought, which in their inhuman tranquillity have overcome the torture of their birth. Textual criticism cannot enable us to construct final answers to textual questions, but it can teach us how to ask the questions in a way that does justice to the capabilities of mind. It puts us on the trail of one class of our monuments and helps us to see the process by which humanity attempts, sometimes successfully, to step outside itself.

Postscript

EACH of the concerns touched on here has been the subject of a voluminous literature, extending back over the centuries, and debates about such issues will continue endlessly, as long as there are minds to address them. Readers who desire suggestions for pursuing what has been said about one or another of these questions may find a useful starting point in the Modern Language Association's *Introduction to Scholarship in Modern Languages and Literatures* (edited by Joseph Gibaldi, 1981), which contains introductory surveys, with reading lists, on linguistics (by Winfred P. Lehmann), historical scholarship (by Barbara Kiefer Lewalski), literary theory (by Paul Hernadi), literary criticism (by Lawrence Lipking), and textual scholarship (by the present writer). For the philosophy of mind, knowledge, and history lying behind the points I have made, one might take up Thomas S. Kuhn's *The Structure of Scientific Revolutions* (1962, 1970), Richard Rorty's *Consequences of Pragmatism* (1982), and—for a collection of essays with extensive reading lists—*Philosophy in History* (edited by

Richard Rorty, J. B. Schneewind, and Quentin Skinner, 1984).

Among the twentieth-century classics of textual criticism are A. E. Housman's preface to his edition of the first book of the *Astronomicon* of Manilius (1903) and "The Application of Thought to Textual Criticism" (1921), both available in his *Selected Prose* (edited by John Carter, 1961) and in his *Collected Poems and Selected Prose* (edited by Christopher Ricks, 1988); R. B. McKerrow's *Prolegomena for the Oxford Shakespeare* (1939); W. W. Greg's "The Rationale of Copy-Text" (1950), available in his *Collected Papers* (edited by J. C. Maxwell, 1966); and Fredson Bowers's *Bibliography and Textual Criticism* (1964) and "Multiple Authority: New Problems and Concepts of Copy-Text" (1972), the latter (and much else of related interest) available in his *Essays in Bibliography, Text, and Editing* (1975). Admirable accounts of the long development of textual criticism as applied to biblical and classical texts are provided by Bruce M. Metzger's *The Text of the New Testament* (1964, 1968), L. D. Reynolds and N. G. Wilson's *Scribes and Scholars: A Guide to the Transmission of Greek and Latin Literature* (1968, 1974), and E. J. Kenney's *The Classical Text: Aspects of Editing in the Age of the Printed Book* (1974). In an essay called "Classical, Biblical, and Medieval Textual Criticism and Modern Editing" (*Studies in Bibliography* 36 [1983]: 21–68), I have tried to offer an overview of this history and to relate it to the textual approaches that have been taken, mostly in the twentieth century, to post-medieval writers. I have also written three essays, now collected as *Textual Criticism since Greg: A Chronicle, 1950–1985* (1987), analyzing the extensive discussions of editorial theory that have occurred since Greg's landmark essay. I mention these pieces of mine because they provide (whether or not one agrees with their judgments) a convenient guide to a large mass of material and because their arguments underlie the rationale presented here.

As one reads through all these works (and the works mentioned in them—and then the works cited in *those* works), one gains an understanding of the cycles of thought through which these several fields have passed. One also comes to see, ever more clearly, that these fields, like all fields, are thoroughly interconnected: all are the products of the human mind. This spaciousness of view puts one in a position to conclude that progress toward understanding—in these endeavors as in others—entails an openness to the various ideas that have served temporarily, each in its turn, to satisfy the persistent human craving for absolute truth.

INDEX